The story of Dragons

The story of Dragons

> Discover the delights of dragons in Eastern and Western culture
>
> SEAN BRAND

Ivy Press

First published in the UK in 2007 by
Ivy Press
The Old Candlemakers
West Street, Lewes
East Sussex BN7 2NZ, UK
www.ivy-group.co.uk

Copyright © 2006 Ivy Press Limited

All rights reserved. No part of this publication may be reproduced or transmitted in any form or by any means, electronic or mechanical, including photocopying, recording, or by any information storage and retrieval system, without permission in writing from the publisher.

ISBN 10: 1-905695-20-9
ISBN 13: 978-1-905695-20-1

Printed and bound in China
1 2 3 4 5 6 7 8 9 10

Ivy Press
This book was conceived, designed, and produced by iBall, an imprint of Ivy Press.

Creative Director Peter Bridgewater
Publisher Jason Hook
Editorial Director Caroline Earle
Art Director Sarah Howerd
Designer Luke Herriott
Picture Researcher Katie Greenwood

Picture Acknowledgements
Bridgeman Art Library/Arni Magnusson Institute: 31R; Kunsthistorisches Museum: 33; Musée Nat. des Arts et Traditions Populaires: 39; Royal Library, Copenhagen: 31L. Corbis: 49; Araldo de Luca: 51; Arte & Immagini srl: 47; Bettmann: 35, 56; Burstein Collection: 7L; Historical Picture Archive: 59; Lindsay Hebberd: 21; Michael Freeman: 20; Museum of M.D. Mallorca/Ramon Manent: 27, 37; Philadelphia Museum of Art: 23; Summerfield Press: 7R. istockphoto: 61. JupiterImages Corporation: 1, 17. Topfoto: 8, 12, 13, 15, 17T, 29L, 43, 44, 45, 48, 53, 55, 60; HIP: 29R; HIP/British Library: 54. Yeo Kian Wah: 24.

Contents

Introduction	6
DRAGONS IN THE EAST	9
Eastern Dragon Lore	10
Ancient Dragons of Mesopotamia	12
Ancient Egyptian Dragons	14
Dragon Kings of China	16
Dragon Pets	18
Naga Kings of India	20
Japanese Dragons of the Deep	22
Chinese New Year	24
DRAGONS IN THE WEST	27
Western Dragon Lore	28
Norse Dragons	30
Ancient Greek Dragons	32
Siegfried and Fafnir	34
Saint George and the Dragon	36
The Turtle Dragon of France	38
English Dragon Legends	40
Western Dragons in History	42
Sea Dragons of the West	44

47	**DRAGONS IN ART AND LITERATURE**
48	Dragon Tales
50	The Laocoon
52	Beowulf and Grendel
54	Merlin's Dragons
56	The Jabberwock
58	The Revival of Chivalry
60	Dragon Symbols
62	Useful Dragon Sources
64	Index

Introduction

The extraordinary thing about dragons is that, despite the fact that they have almost certainly never existed, they are instantly recognizable to children and adults around the world. They lie deep in the collective culture of humankind, and draw out fear, fascination, and horror, in different measures according to where you live. Their constituent parts—reptilian, fire-breathing, winged, and clawed—are similar almost everywhere. But their meaning and associated stories vary widely from region to region, as do the particulars of their appearance and character.

When we think of dragons in Europe, an evocative picture immediately springs to mind: green scales, wings, fiery breath, hidden away in a distant and inaccessible lair. That is the image inspired by the pictures and statues of Saint George and the dragon.

Introduction

[Far left] *Engraving of a winged dragon, taken from Konrad Gesner's* Historia Animalium *published 1551-1558.*

[Left] *A fifteenth-century view of St. George and the Dragon by Carlo Crivelli.*

[Right] *Hercules kills the Hydra, as seen by Antonio Pollaiolo, ca. 1480.*

The first work of literature produced in the British Isles probably some time in the eighth century CE—the epic poem *Beowulf*—included a description of a "smooth, spiteful dragon that flies through the night, enveloped in flame." This dragon was described as a "worm," living in a remote burial mound for 300 years, and boiling the streams with its fiery breath.

In 1937 the Anglo-Saxon scholar J.R.R. Tolkien published his children's book *The Hobbit*, in which he described his own creation, the dragon Smaug, as deadly and greedy for gold and jewels.

Dragons have been associated with sea serpents, with ancient memories of dinosaurs—however unlikely—and even with strange lights in the sky. And, as well as the

Introduction

[Above] *An Eastern dragon with the sea as a background, from the ceiling of the Haw Par Villa in Singapore.*

traditional description, there are references to eagle's feet, batlike wings, lion's forelimbs, reptile's heads, fish's scales, and antelope's horns.

An outsider might imagine therefore that Western dragons should inspire only fear and revulsion. Yet they also possess an awe-inspiring and terrible kind of beauty. Far from shunning the very idea of dragons, heroes and nations have both wanted to be associated with them. They have been considered the embodiment of power and courage: both Roman and ancient Persian soldiers marched into battle carrying dragon banners, and when Emperor Constantine II entered Rome in 357 CE, he was preceded by a series of gigantic dragon standards.

In the Far East, dragons have many of the same characteristics as in the West, but they are overwhelmingly regarded as positive harbingers of good fortune. Eastern dragons are sometimes associated with treasure, and sometimes even eat maidens, though they do not generally fly or breathe fire. In fact, Eastern dragons are primarily associated with the water element, bringing prosperity and long life. They rule over oceans, storms, and rivers and their life-giving properties are apparent at Chinese New Year.

Dragons appear in myths about the creation of the world in ancient Mesopotamia and Egypt as well as in Norse legends. This elemental creative power lies behind both the fear and the compelling attraction of dragons. They provide godlike images of creation and destruction, but they are also—at least in the West, with their rage, greed, and stench—reflections of ourselves, of humanity gone wrong.

DRAGONS IN THE EAST

Eastern Dragon Lore

Considering the dragon is a fantastical beast that does not exist (or so the zoologists say), it is strange that schoolchildren in China would describe one in much the same way as their counterparts in London, Paris, or New York. Stranger still, the characteristics they would come up with today are very similar to ones they would have come up with two thousand years ago.

The fierce jaws, the fiery breath, the wings, and the reptilian tails are familiar in ancient stories in both West and East. But, while Western dragons tend to be greedy and destructive, Eastern dragons are more elemental and more benevolent.

For those of us brought up in the West—and taught to regard dragons with terror and loathing—the brilliant, wise, and lucky dragons of the East can come as a surprise. The Eastern variety tend to be luck-creating, angelic creatures that bring fortune and wealth. They bring rain and storms—the keys to prosperity in the ancient world.

Eastern dragons include the blue dragons of the air, dragons that guard buried treasure, and dragon kings that preside over oceans, rivers, and storms. As well as providing an emblem for the Chinese emperors, who wore magnificent golden dragons on their tunics, they are particularly associated with water. They are linked with the rain that is vital for producing the rice harvest.

COLORED DRAGONS

Chinese dragons appear in specific colors according to their function and significance.

- *Black dragons are symbols of the north and cause storms.*

- *Blue dragons are symbols of the east and are a sign of the arrival of spring.*

- *Red dragons also cause storms, and are symbols of the west.*

- *White dragons are symbols of the south and a sign of death—which is not bad in Chinese culture, but rather a sign of renewal.*

- *Yellow dragons are imperial dragons and are deeply revered.*

[Right] *The color of a Chinese dragon will tell you what it does or represents and which point of the compass it rules.*

Eastern Dragon Lore

There are dragons at every level of Eastern mythology, from the commander of the river dragons, Chien-Tang, to the huge Pa snakes that eat elephants and finally disgorge their bones three years after the meal.

Eastern dragons are even today the objects of great respect: a major advertising campaign by an American sneaker manufacturer was abandoned in China recently because so many people complained about the representation of the dragon.

THE STORY OF FU HSI

Fu Hsi was one of the mythological first emperors of China, living about 2800 BCE. On the bank of the Yellow River he met a dragon-horse that had strange markings on its back. The dragon taught him writing based on these markings, and also all the other prerequisites of civilization: numbers, fishing, domesticating animals, and how to use a set square.

Dragons in the East

ANCIENT DRAGONS OF MESOPOTAMIA

The oldest literature in the world, the mythology of ancient Mesopotamia, describes how the creation of the world involved dragons. The story goes that the mother of all living things was a fantastic dragon called Tiamat, the female spirit of the whole universe. Her first litter was a whole family of gods, who became increasingly difficult and rebellious, so much so that by the time they had grown up their father had decided to despatch them all. But they heard of his plans, captured him, and killed him. In revenge for this, Tiamat gave birth to a monstrous family of dragons and demons, including scorpion men, fish men, and monstrous dogs, who plagued the lives of the gods.

Ancient Dragons of Mesopotamia

[Left] *Tiamat, shown under attack by Marduk, represented the female principle in the Assyrian creation story.*

[Opposite] *The Musrussu dragon, the symbol of the god Marduk, from an ancient Babylonian boundary stone.*

Eventually, one of the gods called Marduk agreed to meet his mother in single combat. After an enormous battle across the sky, he called the winds of heaven to help him by flying into her mouth. He then killed her and the dragons she had given birth to, and used her ribs to form the vault of heaven, and her skin to create the world.

The story was told in Sumeria, the ancient civilization around the city of Babylon in modern Iraq, about 3000 BCE. Priests used it to explain not only the creation of the world, but also how its creation depended on some power that could keep the great forces of chaos in check.

WERE DRAGONS FEMALE?

In Chinese mythology there are both male and female dragons. In the West there is evidence that dragons were used in some periods as symbols of rampant female sexuality. Feminist writers have recently identified the story of the killing of Tiamat by her son as the moment when humanity rejected the power of women for the rule of men.

Dragons in the East

ANCIENT EGYPTIAN DRAGONS

The ancient Egyptians told a dragon legend that seems to have spread all over the world in different forms. It also goes to the roots of human existence because it explains the daily rising of the sun. The dragon in question was Apep, the ancient Egyptian Satan, but also the personification of chaos. He was represented as much like a gigantic snake as a dragon, and sometimes also as a crocodile. According to the legend, Apep was believed to pursue the sun across the sky every day, and battle the sun god Ra throughout the night. Every night, Apep is killed by trickery and cut into pieces, and when morning comes again, the sun rises. However, soon the pieces are back together again, and Apep is flying through the heavens ready for another battle. All across ancient Egypt, the priests in the temples would pray that Ra would defeat Apep and that the sun would rise.

Every year the priests held a special ceremony that involved building an enormous effigy of Apep, representing everything that was wrong with Egypt, which they then destroyed. They even had a guide called the *Book of Overthrowing Apep* to help them ensure that day followed night—especially in such terrifying moments as eclipses when Apep looked as though he might be getting the upper hand.

[Left] *The sun rises again over the pyramids, having defeated Apep once more.*

Ancient Egyptian Dragons

[Above] *The sun god Ra chops the dragon Apep into pieces.*

BIBLICAL DRAGONS

The Egyptian dragon model found its way into the Bible in the shape of Leviathan and the great sea monster that features in the Book of Job. An important serpent also appears at the end of the New Testament—a massive red dragon with seven heads is seen in a vision by Saint John the Divine in the Book of Revelation, which was eventually "bound and cast into a bottomless pit for a thousand years."

Dragon Kings of China

China boasts many kinds of dragon—sky dragons, fire dragons, wise dragons, and treasure dragons—and most importantly water dragons. Special ceremonies are held to celebrate dragons on the first and fifteenth of every month, and you will find altars and shrines to dragons all over the Far East—mainly by the sea or rivers.

Chinese dragons preside over anything watery, and they can live in the ocean, fly up across the heavens, and coil themselves around mountains. Water dragons also control the rain. Although they live under water in crystal palaces, they have the power to cause storms, droughts, or floods by fighting in heaven. Even the more minor dragon kings can cause mischief and make your roof leak if you are not careful!

Water dragons are also known as dragon kings. There are four of these in Chinese literature, and they are the brothers who control the four oceans of the world—Ao Chin (South), Ao Jun (West), Ao Kuang (East), and Ao Shun (North). Farmers are urged to watch the behavior of the dragons because this can help them foretell the weather, and they particularly need to placate Ao Kuang, the king of the dragon kings.

DRAGON DEVELOPMENT

Chinese dragons are not just born. They have to grow. They are hatched as water snakes, and, after a thousand years, they will grow fish scales, and then horns. Only at 3,000 years old will a dragon finally develop wings. Fully grown dragons often have the following bizarre set of characteristics: demon eyes, camel heads, cow ears, stag horns, lizard necks, eagle claws, tiger feet, and carp scales. Most of them also have four claws. Only the emperor's dragons, the great yellow dragons that you see on imperial clothing and insignia, have five claws.

Dragon Kings of China

[Above] *A Chinese water dragon—these fearsome creatures have the power to bring rain and thunderstorms.*

[Left] *A Chinese river: home of the dragon kings.*

DRAGON PETS

A thousand years ago, in the time of the Tang emperors in China, or so the story goes, there was a garden in the capital city of Ch'ang-an owned by a nobleman. In his menageries were pandas from Tibet, as well as golden pheasants, yaks, and tigers. There was also—in a large pool of water—a pair of pet dragons, one with blue scales and one with red.

These dragons were fed on roast cormorant and pig, and became tame and fat. One day, they were seen by a wild dragon flying past and warned that, unless they escaped, they would become corrupted by their situation, just like people. The complacent pet dragons failed to heed the warning, so when the palace was attacked, the pet dragons were captured and eaten.

Often the reason why people wanted to keep dragons was because of their wisdom—they needed to ask their advice. One such person was a thirteenth-century Cambodian king who lived in a golden tower together with the actual ruler of the country, which was a dragon with nine heads. But if you are keeping a dragon pet for advice, then—so the legend goes—you need to be careful. If you ask but fail to take their advice, they get angry. In those circumstances, there are luckily a few things that Chinese dragons are afraid of: centipedes, beeswax, and silk that is dyed in five colors.

Another problem with keeping pet dragons is what to feed them. Chinese dragons are particularly known for eating swallows. One emperor of the Sung dynasty kept a purple dragon in his palace, fed on swallows, in order to use its purple saliva as ink.

THE STORY OF THE DRAGON'S PEARL

A story from Szechwan province concerns a little boy who found one of the pearls that dragons keep in the folds of skin underneath their chins. He put it in a rice jar, which then magically began to fill up with food. When the village chief tried to steal the pearl, the boy hid it in his mouth and accidentally swallowed it. There were rumbles and flashing lights, and he turned into a dragon and flew away.

[Right] *Chinese dragons are said to carry a magic pearl in the folds of skin at their throat: these two dragons are guarding a giant pearl too large to fit under the chins of either.*

Dragons in the East

NAGA KINGS OF INDIA

Most Indian dragons are a diverse group of dragon snakes called Nagas. The name means "snake," and these dragons have great hooded heads like cobras. Across the East, there are different but related stories about Nagas. Malay sailors have stories of Nagas with many different heads, and in Thailand they are enormously rich gods of the underworld. In India, the Naga kings rule over water and live in wells or deep pools.

According to Indian legend, a great storm arose one day when the Buddha was deep in meditation next to a lake. Seeing the Buddha's predicament, a Naga king called Mucelinda crept out of the lake in which he lived, wrapped himself around the Buddha seven times to protect him, and spread seven of his heads over the Buddha like an umbrella. When the storm was over, Mucelinda assumed a human form, bowed to the Buddha, and returned to the lake. This legend shows that

Naga Kings of India

DRAGONS AND DOVES

When medieval naturalists in Europe began to write about dragons, they believed that dragons spent a great deal of their time waiting under perindeus trees that were found only in India. Perindeus trees produce fruit that attracts doves, and dragons find doves particularly tasty. Even so, dragons could not risk coming too close to the perindeus trees, because the trees' shadows alone were capable of causing harm, even death.

the Naga kings may be helpful to human beings and that they can take other shapes, too.

Indian mythology also gives us Vitra, a dragon that rules over the monsoon. This evil dragon refuses to release its store of life-giving water until it is hit by lightning from the weather god Indra. There is also an eleven-headed dragon called Ananta, that serves the Indian god Vishnu by offering its long back for the god to rest on.

[Far left] *The Buddha, protected by an Indian Naga king.*

[Above] *A mural of Vishnu, resting against the eleven-headed Ananta.*

Dragons in the East

Japanese Dragons of the Deep

If you have the misfortune to stray too close to a Japanese dragon, you need to take care. Although Japanese dragons are like their Chinese cousins, ruling over water and air, they are much more dangerous (and tend to have three claws rather than the traditional Chinese four).

In Japanese culture, dragons also have a close relationship with turtles—both living in the sea. Turtles are often portrayed as the messengers of dragons, who in turn sometimes take the shape of turtles. Like Western dragons, Japanese dragons—called *Tatsu*—also have a predisposition to insist on maidens for their sacrifices.

One story, about a warrior exiled by an ailing emperor to the Oki islands in the Sea of Japan, has many parallels with Western dragon myths. The emperor's daughter Tokoyo follows the warrior to the island, but fails to reach it because the local fishermen are afraid of the dragons living there. So she steals a fishing boat, rows for days, and falls asleep in a strange shrine on the island. When Tokoyo awakes, she discovers a white-clothed maiden and her weeping parents on the cliffs, and learns that the maiden is about to be sacrificed to the dragon Yofuné-Nushi, who rules over storms. Tokoyo offers to take her place, dives to the bottom of the sea with a dagger between her teeth, and kills the dragon. She then finds a cursed statue of the emperor in the dragon's lair. When the statue has been cleansed and thrown back into the sea, the emperor recovers, and everyone lives happily ever after.

DRAGONS AND JAPANESE EMPERORS

Just as they do in China, Japanese dragons have strong connections to imperial power. In fact, Japanese emperors claim their descent from dragons, which—because they can change shape—can actually mate with human beings. The present emperor Akihito traces his descent back 126 generations to the dragon Princess Fruitful Jewel, a daughter of the dragon king of the sea.

[Right] *Dragons in the clouds: Japanese dragons also rule over the air.*

Dragons in the East

CHINESE NEW YEAR

In Chinatowns in Western cities all over the world, and certainly in cities in China, Chinese New Year is a period of firecrackers, heaving street markets, calligraphy and porcelain stalls, and delicious food—as well as processions of dancing, acrobats, martial arts, traditional Chinese music, and, of course, dragons.

Beautifully painted paper dragons are the centerpieces in what are increasingly popular multicultural celebrations. The dragon dance marks the highlight of the New Year processions every year, as young men hold a dragon made of paper, silk, and bamboo above their heads and dance through the streets.

The Chinese New Year is always celebrated on the second new moon after the winter solstice—the first new moon of the year under the lunar calendar—which can be as early as January 21, or well into February. New Year means turning over a new leaf, starting afresh, and cleaning the house from top to bottom. In Chinese culture, it is also traditionally a time for family reunions.

The traditional lantern festival, when the dragons appear on the streets, takes place on the fifteenth day of the new moon. This is when everyone is supposed to dress in red. Dragons play a prominent role because they are symbols not just of divine protection but also of good fortune. Dragons can ward off evil spirits and protect the vulnerable, and at New Year they are called upon to do so.

[Above] *The distinctive tail of a dragon on the streets at Chinese New Year.*

[Right] *A magnificent paper dragon's head at a New Year celebration.*

DRAGONS AND THE FIVE ELEMENTS

The Chinese horoscope has a cycle of 60 years. This means the sign you were born under appears only once every six decades—you will probably experience a repeat year of your exact sign only once in a lifetime. Dragons are divided into the five different Chinese elements (metal [such as gold], water, wood, fire, and earth):

Golden Dragons *(most recent year: 2000) are enormously wealthy and successful but can be inflexible and bullheaded. The birthrate in China leaps by as much as ten percent in Golden Dragon years.*

Water Dragons *(most recent year: 1952) are hopelessly optimistic, but are less driven than the other dragons. They are good negotiators and more generous.*

Wood Dragons *(most recent year: 1964) are creative, imaginative, brave, and outspoken. They think up brilliant new ideas and have the nerve and the determination to put them into practice.*

Fire Dragons *(most recent year: 1976) are intolerant and short-tempered, completely determined, and able to build empires, and inspire followers to help them to do it.*

Earth Dragons *(most recent year: 1988) are just as determined but more patient. They plan for the long haul and are farsighted and cooperative.*

YEARS OF THE DRAGON

In Chinese astrology, the Dragon years come around every twelve years and are especially auspicious. Recent Dragon years have been 1928, 1940, 1952, 1964, 1976, 1988, 2000. Those born in the Year of the Dragon are generally self-confident, decisive, and commanding, like an emperor, but can also be temperamental, destructive, and stubborn.

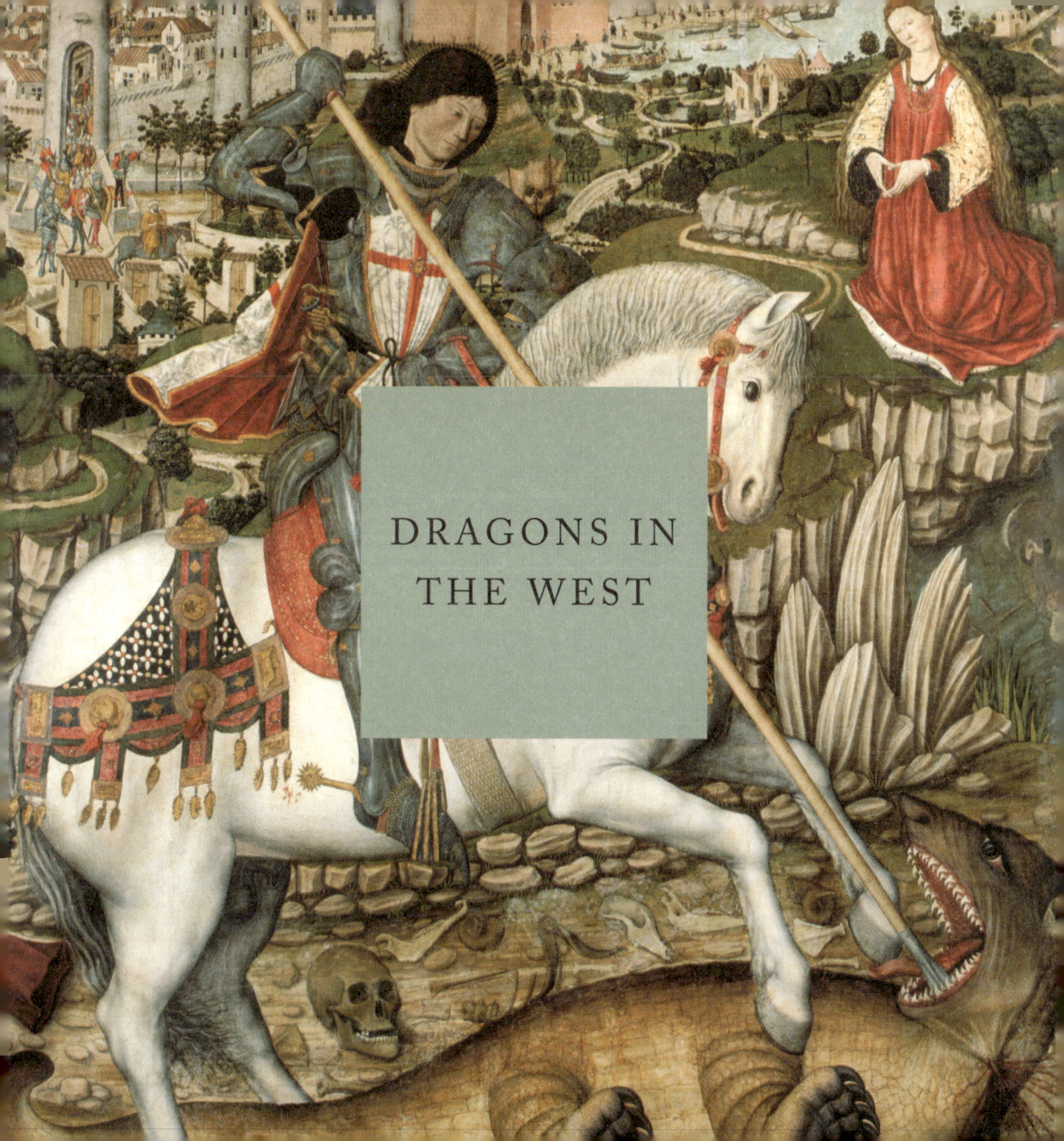

DRAGONS IN THE WEST

Western Dragon Lore

When the seventeenth-century antiquary William Stukeley investigated the extraordinary stone circle in Avebury in the English countryside, he realized that originally—before so many of the stones had been removed—they had been arranged in the shape of an enormous serpent, as a monstrous temple to the sun.

All over the world, and throughout early history, dragons were symbols of elemental power. As in the ancient Egyptian myth of Apep, they were responsible for moving night into day. In Christian Europe, however, these powerful symbols developed differently. The font in the medieval church in Avebury incorporates a twelfth-century carving of a battle between a dragon and a bishop. More than 3,000 years after the stone circle had been built, dragons had become symbols of something else: the darkness at the heart of the old world, whether sexuality or another kind of elemental power or superstition, which the new church must overcome.

Like Eastern dragons, Western dragons come in a range of categories. There are serpentine cockatrices that kill with a direct look; two-legged wyverns; and dragons with the heads of eagles, known as griffins. Unlike Eastern dragons, the Western variety is more down-to-earth. Western dragons are troublesome, sometimes murderous, greedily obsessed with gold and laying waste the surrounding countryside. Often, in Western legends, they start as young and harmless, sometimes on a simple diet of milk. Some start life as a different creature altogether, like the dwarf-turned-dragon Fafnir in Norse mythology.

The heroes and heroines who fight dragons are also integral to the stories. They are usually noblemen but sometimes servants. Others are saints. Sometimes they use traditional and chivalric methods, often aided by magical advice or other support. Sometimes, on the other hand, they resort to trickery in the form of mirrors, or the more immediate effect of explosives. There are even those who manage to get inside the dragon and destroy their internal organs.

Western dragons, however, are not purely demonized figures; their image is used to represent institutions from monarchies to bars to give the impression of power and courage.

Western Dragon Lore

[Above] *St. Michael the archangel battling a many-headed beast and (right) dressed like a knight. Unlike their Eastern counterparts, Western dragons are seen as greedy and fearsome creatures to be destroyed rather than symbols of good fortune.*

EAST EUROPEAN DRAGONS

In Russia and Eastern Europe, dragons—known as zmey *or* smok *in Belarus—are fire-breathing, greedy, and murderous creatures, with seven heads that grow back if they are cut off. Their blood is so poisonous that even the ground is unable to absorb it. The most famous dragon in the region was the Wawel, which lived in caves near ancient Krakow in Poland. It was killed by a boy who persuaded it to eat sulfur and tar, after which it became so thirsty that it drank until it burst.*

Norse Dragons

The whole universe was held upright by a vast ash tree known as Yggdrasil, the "world tree," according to Norse mythology. Unlike the mythology of the East, there were no dragons involved in the creation of the world in Northern European myths. Yggdrasil grew by itself out of the chaotic void before creation. But it was threatened by a terrifying dragon called Nidhoggr, who gnawed at the roots of the tree (and will go on doing so until the end of the world).

Nidhoggr was frustrated by the three Norns, who wove the webs of fate for the world above, and who watered the tree every day from a magic well and restored it. But that is not the end of the story. One of the Norse gods, Loki, fell from grace and gave birth to a family of monsters who threatened the world. There was Hel, the goddess of the underworld, a fearsome wolf called Fenrir, and a dragon serpent called Midgard. Fed by a goat which gnawed the branches of Yggdrasil, the other gods battled with these hideous creations, binding Fenrir in irons and banishing Midgard to the deepest part of the ocean, where its writhing caused storms and tempests. (From there, it will break out to devastate the earth at the end of time.)

The god Thor made one more attempt to deal with the dragon. He dangled the head of an ox on a chain into the sea. Midgard took the bait, and Thor raised his hammer to strike but the giant Hymir—his assistant—lost his nerve, cut the chain, and the dragon escaped.

THE STOOR WORM

The closest creature to a dragon in Norse mythology in Britain is the gigantic Stoor Worm from the Scottish Orkney Isles. The worm was so big that it coiled all around the Earth, and demanded seven virgins from the islanders every week in tribute. The worm was killed by Assipattle, who allowed himself and his boat to be swallowed by the dragon; he sailed down its intestines, and dug some burning peat into its liver.

Norse Dragons

[Above] *The wolf Fenrir with the "world tree" Yggdrasil.*

[Left] *Thor wields his hammer as he fishes for the dragon Midgard.*

Ancient Greek Dragons

Often when Greek gods and goddesses bred with each other, the resulting offspring were monsters, like Cerberus or the Sphinx. Styx and Pallas are said to have produced a dragonish lizard with a hundred heads called the Hydra. The task of slaying it was one of the labors given to the hero and demigod Hercules. His problem was that whenever he cut off one of the heads, three more would grow in its place. It was only by setting fire to the forest, and cauterizing each wound, that Hercules was finally able to kill the beast. Hercules was therefore experienced when he found himself fighting a similar monster in the Garden of the Hesperides, and battling an enormous sea dragon to which the daughter of the King of Troy, Hesione, was about to be sacrificed.

Another Greek hero, Perseus, was asked by the King of Ethiopia to save him and his people from a similar sea dragon. Perseus arrived in time to save the king's daughter, Andromeda, who had been chained to a rock to await her fate. Perseus thus featured in one of the first of many dragon stories in which heroes save princesses and receive a lucrative marriage and extensive property as a reward.

JASON AND CADMUS

Among Greek heroes who faced dragons with varying degrees of success, and who often planted dragon's teeth in the ground to grow into men, were Jason and Cadmus. Accompanied by Medea, the daughter of the King Aeetes of Colchis, Jason once had to creep past a sleeping dragon in order to take possession of the Golden Fleece. Cadmus, for his part, killed a sacred dragon, planted its teeth, and employed the men who grew up as a result to build the city of Thebes. But he never quite escaped the bad luck from the encounter with the dragon. He inadvertently wished to become a dragon himself—then he grew scales and changed into the shape of the serpent he had killed.

Ancient Greek Dragons

[Left] *Giuseppe Cesari portrays Perseus rescuing Andromeda in the nick of time.*

Siegfried and Fafnir

The author of *The Lord of the Rings*, J.R.R. Tolkien, revived the ancient northern myth detailing the greed of dragons and their love of gold. Nowhere is this link made more obvious than in the story of Siegfried, or Sigurd as he was also known, the Teutonic hero who appears in the Icelandic *Volsunga Saga* and later in so many of the operas of Richard Wagner.

Siegfried faces a series of temptations by his foster-father, culminating when he is told the fantastical story of the Otter's gold, guarded by the dragon Fafnir—a dwarf whose greed had transformed him into a dragon. After a great deal of advice from his foster-father, who tells him that bathing in Fafnir's blood will grant him invulnerability, Siegfried digs a series of pits to drain the dragon's blood and lies in wait. He eventually manages to plunge a dagger—forged from the shards of his father Sigmund's old sword—into Fafnir's breast. He then washes in the dragon's blood, knowing that this will make him invulnerable. But, just as Achilles remains vulnerable in his heel, Siegfried is left with a vulnerable spot on his shoulder when a leaf falls on it and prevents it receiving protection from the dragon's blood. Siegfried then drinks the dragon's blood and finds he can talk to the birds, who warn him that in fact his foster-father is trying to kill him.

After many other exciting adventures, Siegfried is eventually killed by his brother-in-law while lying in bed with a shoulder wound.

DRAGON SHIPS

Norse warriors used dragons as symbols of war. For nearly three centuries, from 800 CE, Viking longships—also known as drakkar—*sailed from Scandinavia as far as North Africa and North America. The biggest ships were up to 100 feet long and could reach speeds up to 14 knots. They all typically heralded their presence by the great carved dragon head at their bows.*

Siegfried and Fafnir

[Left] *Siegfried wields the fatal blow for Fafnir.*

Saint George and the Dragon

The process by which Saint George—originally a senior officer in the Roman Army—became the quintessential dragon-slaying hero is now lost in the mists of time. He is supposed to have been born in Asia Minor or Palestine and to have objected to the Emperor Diocletian's orders to carry out a serious persecution of local Christians, because he was himself a Christian. As a result of his objection, he was allegedly tortured and put to death in 303 CE.

Churches dedicated to Saint George began to appear less than a generation after his supposed death, though there is little evidence that he ever actually existed. As the cult of Saint George evolved, however, he was transformed into a Christian knight, wearing a red crusader cross. It was as a warrior hero that he became the patron saint of England, Genoa, and many other places (as well as, incidentally, the patron saint of skin disease).

The first mention of a dragon in connection with Saint George was not until the thirteenth century, when the story arose that—like Perseus—he had rescued a king's daughter who was about to be handed over to a dragon. The story was set somewhere in what is now Libya, but which was originally Roman agricultural land. He then either killed the dragon himself or led it tamely into the town, and refused to kill it until the people who lived there became Christians.

Saint George is no longer an official saint in the Roman Catholic calendar, but in medieval England his saint's day (April 23) also marked days of celebration and procession with plays, Morris Men, and mummers.

SAINT MICHAEL AND THE DRAGON

In the Bible, the equivalent of Saint George is Saint Michael, the archangel who led the army of heaven in the fight against the dragon in the Book of Revelation. All over Europe, churches such as Mont Saint Michel in France and St Michael's Mount in England that are located on hills and mountaintops—the traditional home of dragons—are dedicated to Saint Michael to this day.

Saint George and the Dragon

[Left] *A Renaissance view of the moment when St. George wins the battle.*

The Turtle Dragon of France

One consistent element of European dragon stories is the potential victim's name. In story after story, she is called Margaret or Martha—like Margaret of Bamburgh in the fearsome story set in Bamburgh Castle in northeast England or the Isle Ste Marguerite in the south of France, which is supposed to have harbored a dragon in the Middle Ages. But the most famous French dragon legend of them all contains a twist—Saint Martha is the heroine who delivers the town from one of the most extraordinary dragons of them all.

The Tarasque had six legs, an armor-plated shell like that of a turtle, and the head of a lion. It burned citizens from the nearby town of Nerluc (the modern Tarascon) with its breath or drowned them by sweeping his tail across the river Rhone, where he lived.

Legend has it that Martha had been preaching in Arles nearby, and arrived in response to requests from the town wearing not armor but white linen. She conquered the dragon with just two burned straws held in the shape of the cross, and some holy water, after which she led it meekly into Nerluc. There, the townspeople pummeled the Tarasque to death, even though Martha begged them to spare the dragon.

Every Ascension Day, effigies of the Tarasque are carried in procession around the modern town of Tarascon—just south of Avignon and very close to the small community of Beaucair (*see below*).

THE DRAC

Strangely enough, the other famous French dragon—known to posterity as the Drac—also lived in the Rhone, but this dragon was invisible to humans. It occasionally left its home deep in the river to take people, and in one story kidnapped a local lavender seller. She nursed its child for seven years before being released, with no memory of where she had been. However, she found she had the power to see the Drac when it stalked the streets of Beaucaire. When the dragon found out, it took out her eyes. The Drac was never killed, and the people of Beaucaire celebrate the legend every June 20 to 22.

The Turtle Dragon of France

[Above] *More like a ferocious turtle than a dragon: the fearsome Tarasque.*

English Dragon Legends

The hero who fights the Lambton Worm, in County Durham in the north of England, was also responsible for the arrival of the dragon in the first place. As a dissolute young man, Lord Lambton had thrown a worm down a local well, and, while he was away on a crusade, the worm had grown to a prodigious size, insisting on the milk of nine cows every day before moving onto a more carnivorous diet.

Lord Lambton consulted a local witch, who advised him to used spiked armor to prevent the worm from squeezing him to death, and to fight it in the middle of a river so that the current would carry the bits of worm away before they could reconstitute themselves.

The plan worked, but in return for the advice he had promised to sacrifice the first creature he encountered after the battle, arranging that a dog would be released to meet him to fulfill the vow. Unluckily, his old father forgot the conditions, and dashed down to the river ahead of the dog. Lambton unfortunately fulfilled the vow and his family was cursed for nine generations as a result.

Like many of their European counterparts, many English dragons have given their name to local landmarks, where dragon-like coil shapes appear in hillsides. Dragon Hill, near Lambton, has to this day ridges that might just have been created by a coiling serpent.

THE DEVELOPMENT OF DRAGONS

The Lambton Worm demonstrates some of the common characteristics of European dragons—their ability to regenerate themselves, their poisonous smell, and also their penchant for milk. But it also introduces a less common idea: dragons growing from quite innocuous creatures. Other dragons generate themselves from piles of dead bodies—like the Norton Fitzwarren Dragon from Somerset, England—but the Lambton Worm starts out just as a worm, like the Mordiford Dragon in Herefordshire, England, that began as the pet of a little girl called Maud.

English Dragon Legends

[Left] *Lord Lambton's spikes on his armor were crucial to his victory over the Lambton Worm.*

Dragons in the West

Western Dragons in History

Written and visual references to dragons through the ages excites our interest but their exact meaning may be difficult to decipher. Cultures mix and divide, and dragons are used in different ages to mean different things. So when you find a reference to dragons, you can't be absolutely sure what is meant. For example, it is recorded that a sixteen-foot serpent was brought to the English city of Durham by an Italian visitor on June 11, 1568. It was known to have killed at least one thousand people before its arrival. History does not relate how or why it left again. But what should we make of the very specific date attached to this legend? Or, indeed, to the story of a dragon appearing in St. Leonard's Forest in Sussex in southern England

> **SPARKLING DRAGONS**
>
> *One old man who died a century ago was recorded as describing a series of beautiful dragons he used to see as a boy near Penllyn Castle in Glamorgan, Wales. They had tails like peacocks and glided above him looking as if they were covered with jewels, he told his interviewer. But he said his father and uncle used to kill them, if they could, because the dragons were "as bad as foxes for the poultry."*

in August 1614—a witness described its features as being more like those of a black and red snake than a serpent.

Some records of dragons refer to genuine beasts that escaped from private menageries. Some dragons—like the Sockburn Worm killed by Sir John Conyers, whose broadsword is still in the library of Durham Cathedral, England—may be folk memories of war expressed in a poetic way. In this case, the Sockburn Worm may have referred to a memory of a traumatic raid by Scottish warriors over the English border in 1143. Some records may be memories of disastrous storms, like the flight of dragons seen flying over London and recorded in the chronicles on November 30, 1222.

However, it is also hard to understand exactly what is meant by references to the winged dragon seen near Lake Lucerne in 1619, or to the webbed-footed dragon examined outside Rome in 1660 by the German traveler Athanasius Kircher. In the case of some reports of dragons, we shall never know their true meanings.

[Above] *More like a massive dog than a lizard: the Moston Dragon.*

[Left] *A dragon—right at the bottom of the Bayeux Tapestry—heralds the invasion of England in 1066.*

Sea Dragons of the West

There is no doubt that reliable sightings of sea dragons are more common, even these days, than glimpses of dragons on land and in the air. Unlike the rumors of dragons on land and in the air, the dragons people meet at sea seem to be taken more seriously by scientists and mariners.

One of the most fearsome sea serpents of legend was the Kraken. More like a giant squid than a dragon, it was said to have been seen off the coast of Norway and Iceland. The Kraken may not have been the truly stupendous monsters described by the Bishop of Bergen in 1752 as like islands a mile and a half across, but they have been recorded as attacking ships, even within living memory.

Continuing surveys in Loch Ness in Scotland, and a huge file of sightings of sea serpents of various kinds over the centuries, are testament to the seriousness with which some people regard the existence of sea monsters. There are notoriously controversial photographs, and even more notorious eyewitness drawings, like that of the massive sea serpent seen by the crew of the British frigate *Daedalus* in the south Atlantic in 1848.

As recently as 1905, two ships within three days of each other reported sighting a sea serpent with a long neck off the Florida coast. One of these ships was an oceanographic research vessel with scientists on board who were astonished to see a fin, six feet in length, rise above the surface of the water.

A SEA DRAGON TORPEDOED

When the German submarine U28 torpedoed the merchant ship **Iberian** *off the Irish coast in 1915, there was an enormous explosion underneath the surface as the ship sank. Amidst the wreckage thrown into the air was what the submarine's crew described as a "gigantic sea mammal," sixty feet long and shaped like a crocodile. The beast is said to have writhed for about fifteen seconds before it sank.*

Sea Dragons of the West

[Above left] *The controversial 1934 photograph of the Loch Ness monster.*

[Right] *A sea dragon as imagined by the artist Gordon Wain in 1890.*

45

Dragons in the West

In 1966, the around-the-world yachtsman Sir Chay Blyth saw a creature—about 35 feet long—dive suddenly underneath his boat. He reluctantly described it as a "sea serpent." At the end of 2004, a Japanese team filmed a giant squid for the first time, nearly 3,000 foot under the sea, and about 26 feet long. It may not have looked like a dragon, but Hercules might still have mistaken it for a distant relative of the Hydra.

Nor are stories of sea monsters entirely distinct from the stories of dragons. The Loch Ness monster has been described by eyewitnesses who encountered it on land. The legend of the Sea Worm of the nearby Solway Firth also describes an ocean-going dragon that fed on the fish stocks—local inhabitants killed it by impaling it on stakes.

[Below] *Ten feet long: the Komodo dragons very much exist.*

REAL DRAGONS

When the news emerged in 1912 that live dragons had been discovered by a fishing expedition to the Indonesian island of Komodo, many people refused to believe it. Yet there they are, up to ten feet in length, flesh-eating, as fast as dogs, and with poisonous saliva. Dragons at least twice that size seemed to have lived in Australia as relatively recently as 20,000 years ago, and the rumors continue that some are still there.

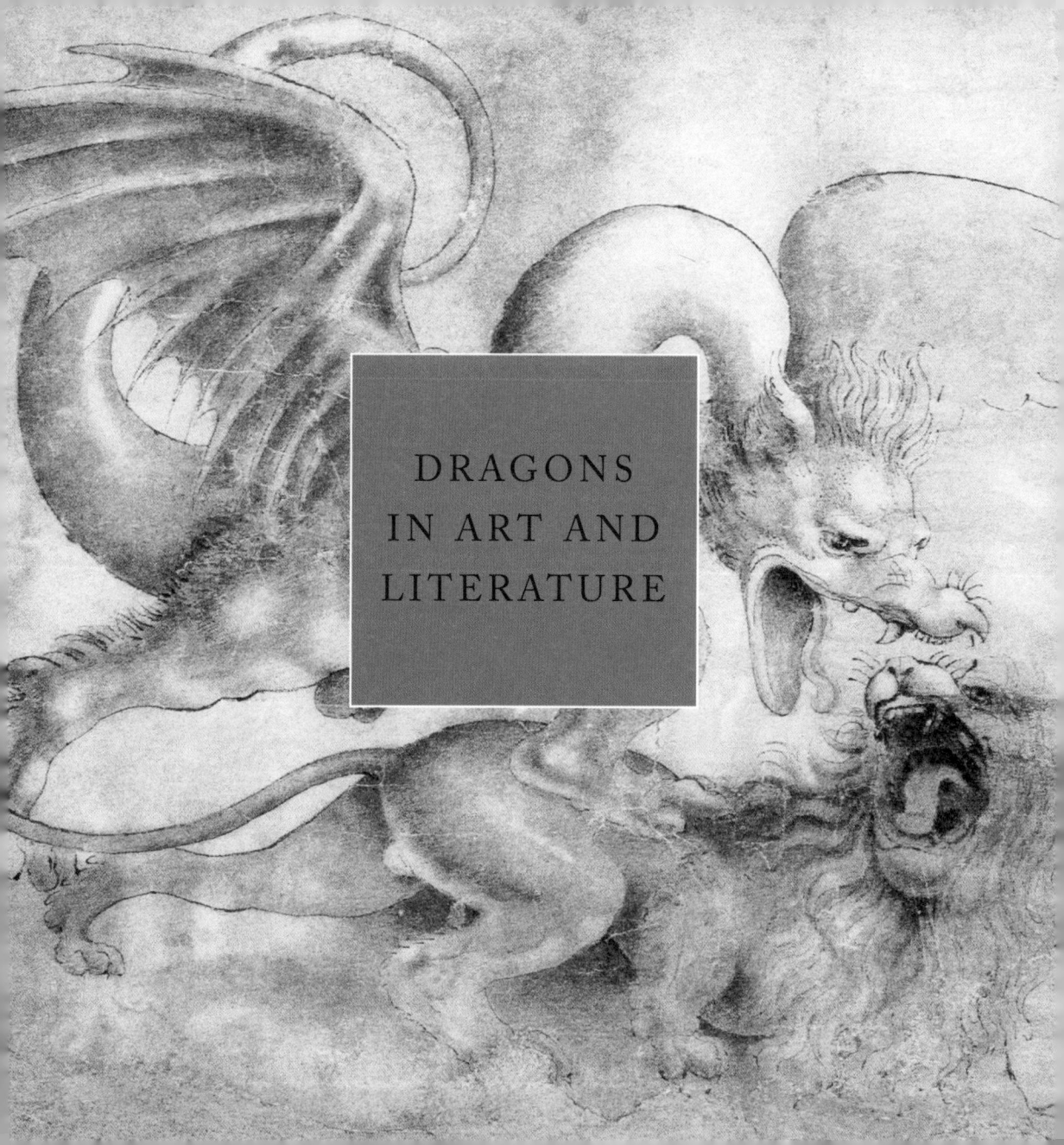

DRAGONS IN ART AND LITERATURE

Dragons in Art and Literature

Dragon Tales

In the British Isles alone, there are over 70 towns and villages with individual stories about dragons. For a creature that never existed, there is remarkable unanimity about what dragons are and how you recognize them. Even the traditional distinctions between the luck-bringing dragons of the East and the destructive dragons of the West seem to be blurring as China opens up to the West and the growth of Chinatowns bring Chinese dragons into western cities.

Yet the layers of symbolic meaning are extraordinarily deep and paradoxical, and as dragons burrow deeper into our consciousness—both in high and popular culture—it is increasingly difficult to pin down their complex levels of meaning.

From *Beowulf*, the oldest surviving literature to emerge out of the British Isles, through Edmund Spenser's *The Fairie Queene* (1882), Wagner's *Siegfried* (1854), and Tolkien's fearsome and greedy dragon Smaug, dragons have been part of all our mental paraphernalia ever since human beings developed a culture. Then there have been the myriad verses, legends, ditties, and songs composed, and the processions and rituals that have taken place—and frequently still take place—all over the world.

Dragon stories were given an added cultural twist by the momentous discovery of the fossils of long-extinct creatures in the nineteenth century, which began to excite the imagination of writers almost within living memory. When fossil footprints two feet across or more are uncovered, as they are every few years, they are categorized these days as belonging to dinosaurs. These discoveries feed into science fiction and fantasy stories that pour forth from publishers every year.

LIGHTS IN THE SKY

From the dragons seen in the sky over London in 1222 CE, to the dragons seen in the north of England some centuries later and described as "bright flying lights," there is a clear relationship between what our ancestors knew as "dragons" and what we now known as Unidentified Flying Objects (UFOs). Like the original dragon legends, Hollywood treatments of UFOs show a similar ambiguity about whether these are harbingers of doom or arrivals of enormous beneficence to humanity. There is the same ambiguity about the meaning of dragons today: symbols of supernatural rage or a glimpse of magic beyond a drab, conscious world?

[Left] *St. George and the dragon again: this time from the frontispiece of an early edition of Spencer's* The Faerie Queene.

[Right] *Siegfried confronts the dragon in the second act of Wagner's opera.*

The Laocoon

One of the most famous marble statues in the world is of a sea serpent attacking the Trojan Laocoon and his sons, as he warns his fellow citizens to "beware of Greeks bearing gifts"—and, in particular, the gift of the wooden horse, which is about to be instrumental in the sack of Troy. The dragon—for that is what this sea serpent was—was sent by the sea god Poseidon, who was supporting the Greeks. But, as Laocoon felt its scaly tentacles around his neck, his fellow Trojans mistakenly interpreted his fate as a just reward for shedding doubt on the wooden horse.

Laocoon's fate was immortalized in marble by a Greek sculptor, probably from Rhodes about 20 BCE. The sculpture was owned by the Emperor Nero, and when it was dug up again in 1506 CE near Nero's palace, by the enthusiastic early archaeologists of the Renaissance, it so thrilled the great sculptors of the day that it changed the way people have sculpted ever since.

Michelangelo was there when the Laocoon was rediscovered, and was enormously impressed by the tremendous scale of the statue, resolving to do something similar himself. The statue remains in the Vatican to this day.

RENAISSANCE DRAGONS

The same year the Laocoon was unearthed, the artist Raphael was at work on his version of Saint George and the Dragon. Although the Renaissance is not known for its penchant for mythological beasts, some of the great names of the period, including Rogier van der Weyden and Paolo Uccello, were drawn to dragons. Perhaps none more so than Leonardo da Vinci, whose notebooks are filled with dragons, and whose identification with them is apparent in the power of his famous sketch "Dragon Attacking a Lion."

The Laocoon

[Left] *Laocoon and his family in the clutches of the tentacles of the sea monster, sent by Poseidon to stop him warning his fellow Trojans.*

BEOWULF AND GRENDEL

The epic poem *Beowulf*, written some time in the eighth century CE, is the oldest existing poem of its kind from Britain, though it in fact describes events somewhere in what is now Denmark and Sweden. It tells of the heroic efforts of a great Scandinavian warrior called Beowulf after his people are attacked by a monster called Grendel. It is not absolutely clear whether Grendel—who is described as a descendant of Cain—is a dragon, but he certainly shares some murderous characteristics with him and he lives in a lake. Beowulf kills Grendel, but is then confronted by the far more terrifying ordeal of a furious assault by Grendel's mother, and he dives into the lake where she lives to finish the task.

Beowulf has received increasing attention in recent years from critics and writers who see a series of meanings in the ancient tale about modern life. Grendel's evil-looking lake is described as "not far from here"—and seems to some modern writers to stand for something we all fear, and which is too close for comfort. Killing the fear is not enough—after all, we have to confront the creator of the thing we fear before we can go on, like Beowulf, to be kings.

To emphasize that Grendel was not quite a dragon—despite the lake and the claws, and despite the serpents which live with him in the lake—Beowulf is eventually killed in a titanic struggle with a real fire-eating "smooth, spiteful dragon" that he subdues before succumbing to his wounds.

DRAGON TREASURE

The dragon that eventually destroys Beowulf is one of those north European dragons with an obsession with treasure. When he is killed, Beowulf's friends take the treasure and bury it with Beowulf's ashes. The story was championed by the author of The Lord of the Rings, *J.R.R. Tolkien—also a leading Anglo-Saxon expert—in a 1936 lecture in which he castigated academics for studying the book only for what it says about the development of language, and for ignoring the importance of the monsters in the story.*

Beowulf and Grendel

[Left] *Was Grendel a dragon? Perhaps he was more like a monstrous human, as shown here as Beowulf cuts off his head. However, Beowulf eventually dies after battling a vicious fire-breathing dragon.*

MERLIN'S DRAGONS

Legend has it that Merlin, the mysterious magician and mentor to the English King Arthur, lived his life backward—so it is not clear whether his youth was at the beginning or the end of his life. One of the earliest legends about his life, written by the twelfth-century historian Geoffrey of Monmouth, concerns his childhood. In the tale, Merlin is consulted by King Vortigern to discover why his new tower at Dinas Emrys, near Mount Snowdon in Wales, collapses every time it is built.

Merlin explains that the tower is built on an underground pool where two sleeping dragons live, one red dragon and one white dragon. In a dream he describes how a battle between these dragons foretells the future, and the coming clash between the Britons and the Saxons. By describing this dream and correctly predicting the existence of the pool, Merlin escapes being sacrificed as a way to keep the tower steady. But the dream comes

KING ARTHUR AND THE DRAGON

King Arthur kills dragons in the legend, but—more spectacularly—so do two of his most famous knights, Lancelot and Tristram. According to one legend, the love potion that binds Tristram so passionately to Iseult was dragon's blood. In both legends, the dragon comes to symbolize the rage or brutal insanity of the hero, which has to be tamed and overcome in order to progress.

Merlin's Dragons

[Opposite] *Merlin underneath Vortigern's tower, revealing the dragons, as seen in a medieval manuscript.*

[Left] *A more recent representation, as Merlin indicates the fighting dragons to the bemused king—and the white dragon takes the red in its jaws.*

true, and the white dragon—representing the Saxons—finally pushes Celtic Christianity into the far north and west of the British Isles.

The same story is told in an older chronicle by the ninth-century historian Nennius, but this time the youth is not Merlin but Arthur's uncle Aurelianus Ambrosius, a historical figure, who was supposed to have charged into battle under the symbol of a dragon (as many of the Roman legions did). Arthur's father, Uther Pendragon, was believed by medieval historians to have used a double-headed green dragon as his own battle symbol.

THE JABBERWOCK

Charles Dodgson was a shy and reclusive mathematician at Christ Church, an exclusive corner of Oxford University. He had an interest in photography and an unorthodox friendship with the college dean's young daughter, Alice Liddell. Out of this relationship emerged two of the great works of English literature, *Alice's Adventures in Wonderland* and *Through the Looking Glass*, which he had published under the pseudonym Lewis Carroll.

Carroll's own dragon creation comes in a nonsense poem in the second of these books. The poem, in which Carroll coined a whole new vocabulary of words, is probably one of the most famous nonsense verses in the English language. Some of the nonsense words in "Jabberwocky," such as "chortled" and "burbled"—the noises made by the monster as it approaches through the "tulgey wood"—have even gone into the language as permanent additions. The Jabberwock itself has inspired

The Jabberwock

a range of films and books, although it played no great role in the original book. It is clearly a classic dragon, with eyes like flame, "jaws that bite and claws that catch." In the original illustration by the artist Sir John Tenniel, the Jabberwock is shown as having wings, scales, and odd eyes like those of a horse. The only rather strange addition, as befits a children's book, is that the Jabberwock wears a waistcoat.

[Opposite] *The Jabberwock itself, as seen by Sir John Tenniel in Alice's adventure* Through the Looking Glass.

[Below] *The Hydra, fought by Hercules: a supposed similarity with a large oak tree was said to have inspired Lewis Carroll.*

One, two! One, two!
And through and through
The vorpal blade went snicker-snack!
He left it dead, and with its head
He went galumphing back.

SOURCE OF THE JABBERWOCK

Some critics suggest that Lewis Carroll was influenced by an ancient oak tree in the Oxford Botanic Gardens that reminded him of the Hydra. It has also been argued that he was influenced by an old German ballad called **The Shepherd of the Giant Mountains**, *in which a boy kills a griffin—half-lion, half-eagle—in a very similar way to the killing of the Jabberwock.*

The Revival of Chivalry

Nearly two centuries ago, chivalry experienced a revival, which was enormously influential on architecture, literature, art, and everyday culture. Beginning with the popularity of the medieval novels of Sir Walter Scott, and the artistic ideas of John Ruskin, pioneers of chivalry developed new versions of medieval gothic and knightly self-sacrifice.

It was a period that led to a renewed fascination with Saint George—the archetypal Christian knight—in battle with the dragon. The dragon represented for Victorians all they feared the most: chaos, greed, and corruption. The pictures of dragons painted during that period are with us still, but the artists may have been unconsciously copying medieval versions—created at the time of the Renaissance—in which dragons had a very specific, but forgotten, meaning.

The medievalist Samantha Riches discovered that pictures of dragons during the fifteenth century had been quite deliberately given female genitalia. While it is true that some of the legendary Western dragons are female—Grendel's mother, for example—and some of them are described as giving birth, the gender of the dragon is irrelevant in most legends. The implication of this Renaissance shift is that artists like Albrecht Dürer, who worked in Germany immediately before the Reformation, saw dragons as symbolic of female sexuality. These artists portray Saint George as having to choose between the beast that is exposing her sexuality and the demure virgin who is threatened; he kills the first and rescues (and sometimes marries) the second.

THE GARDEN OF EDEN

The story of the Garden of Eden should help us understand why the attitudes to dragons seem to be so different in the West than in the East. Like the creature that tempts Adam and Eve and leads to the fall of man, dragons are serpents. What is more, the same artists in pre-Reformation northern Europe—like Lucas Cranach the Elder—were increasingly portraying the serpent in the garden as female, and sometimes even as a woman like Eve.

[Left] *A renewed version of St. George: manliness as the Victorians saw it.*

Dragon Symbols

When knights rode into battle wearing metal visors, the visors made them unrecognizable, so from the twelfth century a complex system of symbolism known as heraldry was developed to help them identify knights in battle. Many knights chose dragons as symbols of power and courage, just as the Roman legions had done before them. Over time heraldic bearings or coats of arms were sometimes designed to include dragons, either because the dragon symbolized royalty or because the bearer was linked with a dragon legend.

Some local heroes have dragons in their coats of arms because legendary ancestors, such as Sir Moris Berkeley, who killed the Bistern Dragon (in Hampshire, England), are supposed to have taken on troublesome local dragons and killed them—and sometimes, as in the case of Sir Moris, died in the attempt. Many dragon killers in British legends are not knights at all, but local laborers or, in the case of Garston who killed the Dragon of Mordiford, even local criminals.

TWO-LEGGED DRAGONS

Many of the beasts which appear in coats of arms are not strictly dragons at all, but two-legged, fire-breathing beasts—more bird than lizard—called Wyverns. Wyverns are usually described as overwhelmingly evil, but families and institutions still choose them as crests, perhaps for their reputation for courage, clear sight, and their capacity for revenge.

Dragon Symbols

WELSH DRAGONS

Most experts believe that the famous red dragon of Wales, visible at rugby matches all over the world, as well as all over the Welsh principality, began as a symbol of Roman rule, because so many Roman cohorts fought under dragon standards. Since then, the dragon has been a symbol of Welsh nationalism—sometimes golden but increasingly red.

Even so, the later hero who was the seafarer and explorer Francis Drake—whose name means "dragon"—chose the dragon symbol for himself when he was awarded his own coat of arms. During the Tudor dynasty of kings and queens in England, when the ruling family came from Wales, the Welsh dragon was incorporated into the English royal coat of arms.

Dragon shapes are carved into medieval churches all over Europe, just as they are chosen for the names of inns and pubs—especially the Green Dragon. Pub names can be up to one thousand years old, and there are Green Dragons all over England. The link with the color green is a peculiar twist to the dragon story, because the Wherwell Cockatrice—a story about a dragon with death-ray eyes that hatched from a duck egg underneath Wherwell Priory in Hampshire, England—was eventually killed by one of the servants at the priory called Green. The land given him as a reward is still known as Green's Acres and is identified in Harewood Forest nearby.

[Above] *The Welsh dragon, in red, white, and green.*

[Far left] *The Venables family crest shows a dragon holding a child in its mouth in memory of another legend. Sir Thomas Venables killed the Moston Dragon in Cheshire, England—just as it was about to swallow a child—by shooting an arrow into its eye.*

Useful Dragon Sources

Ten Best Dragon Books

1. *Big Book of Dragons, Monsters, and Other Mythical Creatures*, E. and J. Lehner (Dover Pictorial Archive, 2004)
2. *The Book of Dragons and Other Mythical Beasts*. J. Nigg (Barron's Educational Series, 2002)
3. *British Dragons*, J. Simpson (Batsford, 1980)
4. *Chinese Dragons (Images of Asia)*, Roy Bates (Oxford University Press, 2002)
5. *Dragonology: The Complete Book of Dragons*, E. Drake and D. Steer (Templar Publishing, 2003)
6. *Giants, Monsters and Dragons: An Encyclopaedia of Folklore Legend and Myth*, C. Rose (W W Norton & Co Ltd, 2001)
7. *Here Be Dragons: A Fantastic Bestiary*, C. and A. Delacampagne (Princeton University Press, 2003)
8. *The Oxford Companion to World Mythology* David Leeming (Ed.), (Oxford University Press, 2002)
9. *St. George: Hero, Martyr and Myth*, S. Riches (Sutton Publishing, 2000)
10. *Treasury of Fantastic and Mythological Creatures: 1,087 Renderings from Historic Sources* R. Huber (Dover Pictorial Archive, 1981)

Ten Best Dragon Websites

1. www.blackdrago.com (general information)
2. www.chinapage.com/dragon1.html (Chinese dragons in Chinese culture)
3. www.crystalinks.com/chinadragons.html (Chinese dragons)
4. www.draconian.com (general information)
5. www.dragonorama.com (general information)
6. www.colba.net/~tempest/ (general information)
7. www.isidore-of-seville.com/dragons/ (full list of links to dragon art and other web resources)
8. www.mysteriousbritain.co.uk/legends/dragons.html (British dragons)
9. www.sommerland.org (general information and artwork)
10. webtech.kennesaw.edu/jcheek3/dragons.htm (general information)

Ten Best Dragon Storybooks
1. *Beowulf* (trans Seamus Heaney), (W W Norton, 2001)
2. *The Book of Dragons*, Michael Hague, story collection, (HarperCollins, 1995)
3. *The Greek Myths*, Robert Graves (Penguin, 1993)
4. *Grendel*, John Gardner (Vintage, 1989)
5. *A History of the Kings of Britain* Geoffrey of Monmouth, Lewis Thorpe (Ed.), (includes the Merlin stories), (Penguin, 1977)
6. *The Hobbit*, J. R. R. Tolkien (Houghton Mifflin, 1999)
7. *Norse Myths*, Kevin Crossley-Holland (Pentheon, 1981)
8. *The Reluctant Dragon*, Kenneth Grahame (Candlewick, 2004)
9. *The Saga of the Volsungs* (trans. Jesse Bycock), (Penguin, 2000)
10. *Smith of Wooton Major*, J. R. R. Tolkien (HarperCollins, 2005)

INDEX

Ananta, Indian dragon 20
Andromeda 32–3
Apep, Egyptian dragon 14, 28

Beowulf and Grendel 7, 48, 52–3
Biblical dragons 15, 36

Chinese dragons 8, 10, 16–19, 22, 24–6
Claws of a dragon 16, 22
Coats of arms 60–1
Cockatrice 28, 60
Colors of dragons 10, 60
Creation, and dragons 8, 13, 20
Cultural dragons 6–8, 47–61

Death, and dragons 10
Destruction, and dragons 8, 10
Dinosaurs 7, 49
Drac, French dragon 38
Dragon book 62–3
Dragon dance 24–5
Dragon kings 10, 16–17
Dragon pearls 18
Dragon pets 18–19
Dragon ships of the Vikings 34
Dragons of the deep 16, 22–3, 44–6
Dragon symbols 60–1
Dragon websites 62

Earth dragons 26
Eastern dragons 7–26
Egypt, ancient 8, 14–15
Eve as dragon 58
Evil spirits and dragons 24
Eyes of a dragon 16

Fafnir 28, 34–5
Fiery breathing 6, 7, 10, 29, 38, 61
Fire dragons 26

George, Saint 6, 7, 36–7, 48–9, 50, 58–9
Golden dragons 26, 60
Good fortune and dragons 8, 10
Greek dragons 32–3
Grendel 52–3
Griffin 28, 57

Healing, and dragons 18
Hercules and the Hydra 7, 32, 57
Historical dragons 18, 42–3
Horns 8, 16
Hydra, 7, 32, 57

Images of dragons, 6–8, 10
Information about dragons, 62–3

Jabberwock 56–7
Japanese dragons 22–3

Kraken 46
King Arthur 54–5
Komodo dragons 46

Lambton Worm 40–1
Lancelot, Arthurian knight 54
Laocoon statue 50–1
Leonardo da Vinci 50
Leviathan 15
Lights in the sky 7, 49
Loch Ness monster 44

Maidens and dragons 8, 22, 30, 58
Marduk 12–13
Margaret/Marguerite 38
Martha, Saint 38
Merlin 54–5
Mesopotamia, ancient 8, 12–13
Michael, Saint 29, 36
Midgard, Norse dragon serpent 30–1
Moston Dragon 43, 60
Mucelinda 20–1
Musrussu Dragon 13

Nagas and Naga kings 20–1
Nidhoggr, Norse dragon 30
Norse dragons 8, 30–1
Norton Fitzwarren Dragon 40

Oceans, and dragons 16, 22–3, 44–6

Pa snakes 11
Perseus and Andromeda 32–3
Prosperity, and dragons 8, 10

Ra, Egyptian sun god 14–15
Red dragons 10, 54–5, 60
Rising sun 14–15
Roman banners 8, 60

Satan 14
Scales 6, 8, 16
Sea monsters 7, 15, 30–2, 44–6, 50–1
Sex and dragons 13, 58
Siegfried and Fafnir 34–5, 48–9
Smaug (*The Hobbit*) 7, 48

Tail 10, 24
Tarasque, French dragon 38–9
Tatsu, Japanese dragons 22
Thor, Norse deity 30–1
Through the Looking Glass 56–7
Tiamat 12–13
Tolkien, J.R.R. 7, 34, 52
Treasure and dragons 7, 8, 10, 52
Tristram, Arthurian knight 54
Turtles and dragons 22, 38–9

UFOs 49
Uther Pendragon 55

Vitra, monsoon dragon 20

Water, and dragons 8, 10, 16–17, 20–1, 22, 26
Wawel, the 29
Wealth, and dragons 10
Weather, and dragons 7, 10, 20
Welsh dragons 60–1
Western dragons 6–8, 10, 27–46
Wherwell Cockatrice 61
White dragons 10, 54–5
Wings 6, 8, 10
Wisdom, and dragons 16, 18
Wood dragons 26
"Worm" dragons 7, 30, 40–1, 42, 44
Wyvern 28, 61

Years of the dragon 26
Yellow dragons 10, 16
Yofuné-Nushi 22